SUPER SPIDERS

CAVE SPIDERS

BY LISA J. AMSTUTZ

PEBBLE
a capstone imprint

Published by Pebble, an imprint of Capstone
1710 Roe Crest Drive, North Mankato, Minnesota 56003
www.capstonepub.com

Library of Congress Cataloging-in-Publication Data is available on the Library of Congress website.
ISBN: 9798875224690 (hardcover)
ISBN: 9798875224508 (paperback)
ISBN: 9798875224652 (ebook PDF)

Summary: An introduction to cave spiders, including how they hunt, where they live, and more.

Editorial Credits
Editor: Ashley Kuehl; Designer: Kay Fraser; Media Researcher: Svetlana Zhurkin; Production Specialist: Whitney Schaefer

Image Credits
Alamy: Design Pics Inc, 13, Nature Picture Library, 10, 12; Capstone: Kay Fraser (spiderweb), cover and throughout; Getty Images: Adrian Eugen Ciobaniuc, 19; Newscom: imageBROKER/Emanuele Biggi, 9, 11, 16, NHPA/Gerald Cubitt, 14; Shutterstock: All Write studio (spiderweb), 4, 8, 12, 18, Anton Starikov, 20 (left), bluejava1, 18, Ekkys, 20 (right), Federico.Crovetto, 5, Henrik Larsson (spider), cover, back cover, 1, Manoj Kumar Tuteja, 4, Marco Maggesi, 15, Pedro Luna, 8, 17; SuperStock: Universal Images, 7; Svetlana Zhurkin: 20 (back)

Printed and bound in China. 6274

TABLE OF CONTENTS

Words in **bold** are in the glossary.

ALL ABOUT CAVE SPIDERS

Look at those long legs! The giant huntsman spider lives in a cave. It is the world's biggest spider. It is as big as a dinner plate. One of the smallest spiders lives in caves too. It is the size of a grain of salt!

More than 1,000 kinds of spiders live in caves. They like places that are dark and damp. We call them cave spiders.

Cave spiders live around the world. They live underground. But some don't live in caves. They live in **burrows**.

A cave can be a good home. It is not too hot or cold. It is not too dry. It is a good place to hide from **predators**.

LIFE IN THE DARK

Dash! A cave spider runs by. Like all spiders, it has eight legs. Its legs are long and thin. They have tiny hairs on them. These help the spider **sense** its **prey**.

The spider is pale. It does not need color. Cave spiders can't see one another. And predators can't see them. The dark hides them.

Most spiders have eight eyes. But not all cave spiders do. Some have six eyes. Some have none! It is dark in a cave. So eyes are not needed.

Cave spiders can still sense light. They stay away from it. Light means outside. Predators can find them outside.

DINNERTIME

Cave spiders hunt or trap prey. But that is hard to do in the dark. So most make **silk** webs. Some are sticky. Some are not.

Some cave spiders spin sheet webs. These are wide and flat. Prey cannot see them in the dark.

Now the spider waits. It may wait a long time. Few animals can live in caves. Food is hard to find. No plants can grow. They need light to survive.

A cave spider doesn't need to eat often. Its gut can hold lots of food. A meal can last for months.

At last, a bug runs into the web. The spider feels the web move. It rushes over. Bite! It sinks in its **fangs**. Its **venom** kills the bug. The bug's insides break down.

The spider wraps the bug with silk. It sucks out the inside. Now it will wait again.

DON'T TOUCH

Most cave spiders are harmless. But a few can bite. It is best not to touch them.

Cave spiders help keep caves clean. They feed on bugs. Other animals feed on cave spiders. They are part of the web of life.

MAKE A SPIDER WEB

What You Need:

- black paper
- glue
- glitter or thread

What You Do:

1. Use glue to draw a web on the paper.

2. Sprinkle it with glitter or lay thread on top.

3. Let the glue dry.

4. Shake off the extra glitter.

SPIDER JOKES

What do spiders order with their burgers?

French flies!

What are young spiders called?

arach-kids

What do you call spiders that just got married?

newlywebs

Did you hear about the friendly spider who starved to death?

He wouldn't hurt a fly.

GLOSSARY

burrow (BUR-oh)—a hole in the ground made or used by an animal

fang (FANG)—the biting part of a spider's mouth

predator (PRED-uh-tur)—an animal that hunts other animals for food

prey (PRAY)—an animal hunted by another animal for food

sense (SENS)—feeling something to learn what's around

silk (SILK)—long, thin threads made by a spider

venom (VEN-uhm)—a poisonous liquid produced by some animals

READ MORE

Brundle, Joanna. *Arachnids*. Minneapolis: Jump!, Inc, 2024.

Owen, Ruth. *Spiders: We're Not Scary—We're Amazing!* Kent, UK: Ruby Tuesday Books, 2023.

Pettiford, Rebecca. *Spiders*. Minneapolis: Bellwether Media, 2025.

INTERNET SITES

Britannica Kids: Spider
kids.britannica.com/kids/article/spider/353800

Kids Discover: Spiders
online.kidsdiscover.com/unit/spiders

San Diego Zoo Wildlife Explorers: Spider
sdzwildlifeexplorers.org/animals/spider

INDEX

ABOUT THE AUTHOR

Lisa Amstutz is the author of more than 150 children's books on topics ranging from applesauce to zebra mussels. An ecologist by training, she enjoys sharing her love of nature with kids. Lisa lives on a small farm with her family.

Pebble Emerge

CAVE SPIDERS

Did you know the world's biggest spider is a cave spider? These creatures live in damp, dark places. Learn more about these fascinating spiders, including their body parts, webs, and how they hunt prey.

READ MORE BOOKS IN THE
SUPER SPIDERS
SERIES

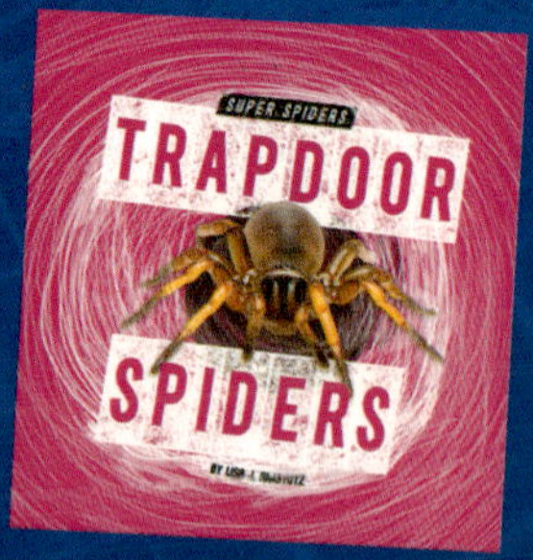

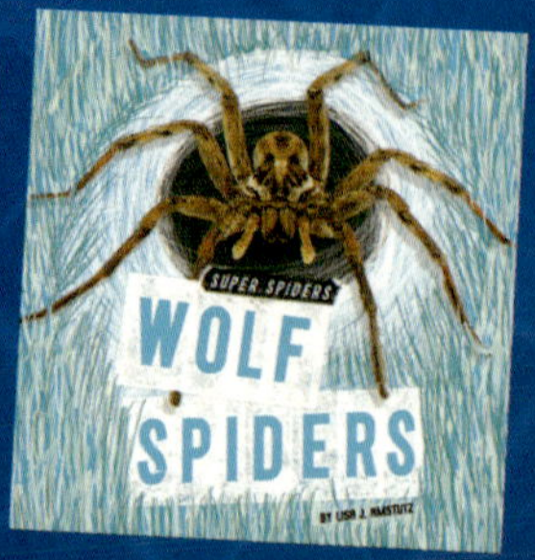

F&P Text Level Gradient™
Officially Leveled by Fountas & Pinnell

capstone
capstonepub.com

$7.99 US / $10.99 CAN
ISBN 979-8-8752-2450-8